M000200211

## PRAISE FOR *THE WARRIOR'S MANTRA*

"I just finished reading *The Warrior's Mantra* by Rodger Ruge, and I recommend it for all serious martial artists. I have long used positive affirmations to heighten my warrior spirit. I have also advised students to use this powerful training technique. But never before have I found a program that provides a concise series of affirmations designed to systematically develop one's warrior mind-set. *The Warrior's Mantra* is just such a program.

Moreover, as a career police officer, Rodger Ruge offers readers a rare insight into the heart and mind of a professional warrior. Drawing from a rich library of personal experience, he illustrates how a real warrior faces life's challenges, great and small, and he seasons his narrative with inspirational maxims from some of history's most notable luminaries.

In closing, *The Warrior's Mantra* is a book every warrior will want to read. I wish Rodger Ruge had written it years ago."

—Forrest E. Morgan, Ph.D., author of
*Living the Martial Way*

"Rodger Ruge has blazed new territory in the field of Warrior Science. His book, *The Warrior's Mantra* provides a superb set of guideposts for those who would walk the warrior's path. Don't just study and learn from this book, make it your mantra!"

—Lt. Col. Dave Grossman, author of
*On Killing* and *On Combat*

"*The Warrior's Mantra* will prepare you as a vigilant "warrior" for the potentially, life-threatening confrontations you experience. Rodger Ruge's years of experience will complete your survival training ... to prepare your mind and spirit for excellence!"

—L. John Mason, Ph.D., owner of
the Stress Education Center

# The
# WARRIOR'S
# MANTRA

# The WARRIOR'S MANTRA

# RODGER RUGE

BOOKS

Fort Lee • New Jersey

Published by Barricade Books Inc.
185 Bridge Plaza North
Suite 308-A
Fort Lee, NJ 07024

www.barricadebooks.com

Copyright © 2005 by Rodger Ruge
All Rights Reserved.

No part of this book may be reproduced, stored in a retrieval system, or
transmitted in any form, by any means, including mechanical, electronic,
photocopying, recording, or otherwise, without the prior written per-
mission of the publisher, except by a reviewer who wishes to quote brief
passages in connection with a review written for inclusion in a magazine,
newspaper, or broadcast.

Library of Congress Cataloging-in-Publication Data

Ruge, Rodger.
   The warrior's mantra / by Rodger Ruge.
     p. cm.
   ISBN 1-56980-284-X (pbk.)
   1. Self-preservation. 2. Affirmations. 3. Men--Psychology. 4. Self-
defense--Psychological aspects. 5. Survivalism. I. Title.

BF697.4S45 2005
158.1--dc22

                                                    2005041062

First Printing
Manufactured in Canada

# Contents

# *Dedication*

This book is dedicated to the select few, the heroes, the warriors who have valiantly committed their lives to protecting the freedoms of our great nation and the lives of our citizens. To assume the role of a warrior, guarding against the wolves that would ravage our society, is among the noblest of actions. To stand with total conviction against evil, in the face of terrible circumstance, is the true measure of one's soul. To those heroes who protect us without conscious thought of reward, but do so out of a sense of duty, honor and principle, I dedicate the passages in this book. Let strength and honor guide your path as a warrior. May God bless you and keep you safe.

> *It is not the critic who counts, not the man who points out how a strong man stumbled or where the doer of deeds could have done better. The credit belongs to the man who is actually in the arena, whose face is marred by dust and sweat and blood; who strives valiantly, who errs and comes short again and again; who knows the great enthusiasms, the great devotions and spends*

*himself in a worthy cause; who at best knows achieve-ment and who at the worst if he fails, at least fails doing greatly, so that his place shall never be with those cold and timid souls who know neither victory or defeat.*

—Theodore Roosevelt,
twenty-sixth president of the United States

# *Acknowledgments*

I would like to acknowledge several people who made this book possible:

**My wife, Peggy, and my daughters, Allyson and Nicole**, for their support and belief in this project. Their love and belief in this book has allowed it to come to fruition.

**George Henry Ruge.** My father, mentor, and friend. Dad has helped me throughout my life to develop the strength of character necessary to challenge myself in a continuing effort toward personal growth. In my youth, I did not always appreciate or understand his guidance, however I now see with the wisdom of years the tremendous effect he has had, and continues to have, on my life. I love you, Dad!

**Ralph Pata.** One of my first partners as a police officer, who helped me to realize being a good cop meant a whole lot more than kicking ass and taking names.

**Jimmy Cook.** The best beat cop I have ever met. A shining example of what a police officer can become in service to his coworkers and community.

**David Anderson.** Dave is my original Wing Chun Kung Fu Sifu (Father), who awakened my warrior spirit.

**Steve Rose.** Steve is my current teacher in the art of Yang Style Tai Chi Chuan. Steve helps me to keep my warrior spirit alive and serves as an endless source of inspiration and challenge. Steve has "been there" as a combat warrior in Viet Nam, and he has my utmost respect as a teacher and trusted friend.

**Kevin Cook.** Kevin is my trusted friend who has continued to help me develop my fighting skills and spirituality. Kevin is a constant source of inspiration and I am always grateful for his insight and wisdom.

**Jim Fraser.** Jim provided the original inspiration for me to write this book through his mentoring during my journey in the P.O.S.T. Master Instructor Development Program.

**Law enforcement, military, and civilian warriors.** To my brothers and sisters, your selfless dedication in keeping our peace and freedom is absolutely essential and must be supported. You allow us all to sleep in peace and freedom. This book is my way of giving something back to those who have taken up the call of the warrior's path.

# Foreword

*Jim Fraser*
*Retired U.S. Army Colonel*

Colin Powell said it best: "Great leaders are almost always great simplifiers. . . ."

Rodger has written a book that has, in a most effective manner, made the mantra a simple and useful tool for all. Best of all, it is an easy read. I had the distinct pleasure of meeting Rodger years ago. Our paths crossed when he was a student in a yearlong instructor development program. This program is by far the most challenging, yet rewarding training program one can participate in as a law enforcement officer in California. Rodger excelled and demonstrated qualities one always strives for, but seldom encounter. He was an exceptional learner and his every endeavor was marked by a commitment to excellence. Quality and excellence were his standards; he did not deviate or accept anything less. Rodger's success as a student was easy to recognize by myself as well as by others. As a result he is one of those chosen to lead this program into the future. This occurs perhaps every five or six years. In my mind it is one of the most significant honors that can be bestowed—to be recognized by those who have developed and parented a highly successful program to carry the torch into the future. With Rodger that decision was easy and we do so knowing the future of the program will be in extremely capable and competent hands.

Rodger's book, *The Warrior's Mantra*, addresses the real issue that is an absolute imperative but seldom receives any training; how does one mentally prepare for the unknown, the difficult, and the stressful challenges a warrior in today's society will face? His mantras offer a simple way to prepare for these challenges and they allow one to do so with ease. Reflecting back on my twenty-seven years as an Army officer I would have found this to be an ideal source book for words of encouragement for me and for those I led. This is a book that should be always at hand, always at the ready, always available; a keeper.

John Boyd, developer of the battle-proven OODA loop got it right when he said: "Machines don't fight wars; terrain doesn't fight wars; humans fight wars; you must get into the mind of humans; that's where the battles are won." Rodger's book addresses issues that those of us who fight today's wars, the military, law enforcement and front-liners in contact with the adversary, must face. The ability to be mentally prepared must be understood and adopted. The battle and the adversary have never been more important or more dangerous. The target is anyone, anywhere, who is an American or supports America. The terrorist has made the battleground one of their choosing. The concern is how do we keep that edge, how do we prepare each and every day for what we might encounter with only a nanoseconds warning? That mental preparation must take place well before the battle. We are obliged by our roles and positions to be mentally and physically prepared at all times. Anything that will provide an edge, give us leverage over that adversary, is vital. Rodger's book is one more tool in our arsenal that will arm us, place on alert, cause us to think and act differently; that difference may be crucial. It could be the distinction between life and death. Read *The Warrior's Mantra*, enjoy it and use it often.

# *Introduction*

*The virtue of perfection is that it is always just beyond the man's reach. That is good. If perfection were attainable then it would have no value—there would be no reason to pursue it.*

—Miyamoto Musashi—*Book of Five Rings*

I have a unique challenge for those of you who would count yourselves among the courageous souls who are defined as warriors, those who battle in the trenches, those who hold the front line and fight to maintain peace. I have designed this book for those warriors who constantly strive to improve themselves—to set themselves apart from the masses.

This book is designed to help you to improve your warrior spirit, as Eastern cultures over the millenniums have done, utilizing the ancient technique of mantras, or positive affirmations. The challenge is to introduce this "new" training technique to the warriors in Western culture who have yet to experience its life-altering power. If you accept the challenge of learning this new technique, I can guarantee you will experience a dramatic and powerful personal transformation as you cultivate and awaken the warrior spirit within you.

A mantra, or affirmation, is a formula of invocation that can deeply affect our ability to succeed. It has the power to alter our lives in ways most of us can scarcely imagine. For the purposes of this book, it is a short phrase that is repeated over and over until it is ingrained in your consciousness. Think of it as planting a small seed in your mind that will grow and flourish until it is an unconquerable and indomitable part of your will. These techniques have been practiced for literally thousands of years with success that is well documented in the annals of history.

Civilizations the world over have used mantras, or positive affirmations, to overcome the most incredible circumstances. When these powerful techniques are combined with the ironclad resolve of willpower, what you will be able to overcome is limitless. Doctors, scientists, and skeptics are left scratching their heads and using words such as "miracle" to explain what science does not yet understand. In the context of this book, the mantras I have listed are designed as positive affirmations to evoke the warrior spirit that exists within each of us. These affirmations have the power to ignite the unconquerable strength of your soul. They will help you to become a powerful force against the evils that lurk in our society.

As a protector of this great nation, you have dedicated your life to a path that can place you in great personal danger. While all animals, *and most people*, would flee from the sound of danger, a warrior goes directly to its source and faces it with steadfast courage. You are the 1 percent of the population who will rise up against those who would attempt to victimize and intimidate our people and our nation. You form a wall of impenetrable protection with your commitment to the warrior's path. While others sleep in peace and freedom, you prowl for the wolves that would attack those unable to defend themselves. Those helpless, timid and beautiful souls depend on your righteous sense of duty for protection. You are the warrior class of our society, as the Samurai were to ancient Japan. Hold your head high, be proud of your chosen path, and never doubt the essential role you play in this world.

Because you never know from day to day what circumstances you will confront, it becomes your personal challenge to do the most you can possibly do to prepare. Having a warrior state of mind, one that is focused on improvising, adapting and overcoming all obstacles, is of supreme importance. This is a challenge you **must** accept in your chosen role as a warrior. To survive, you must be able to face life-altering events in a moment's notice and without the slightest hesitation. This book is designed to help you develop the proper mental attitude. The affirmations will aid you in succeeding even when you are faced with seemingly impossible circumstances. Consider this training a form of exercise designed to keep your subconscious mind in shape, totally prepared for whatever may come. Mental exercise is at least as important as physical exercise and skill building when it comes to enhancing your performance in crisis situations. With the body and mind as one, you will be able to take action as a warrior and succeed.

This book is not designed as a "quick read." To obtain the greatest benefits, I would recommend the following:

Each day, pick one page from the book, and read the short mantra at least three times. Commit this positive warrior affirmation to memory until it becomes deeply ingrained in your consciousness. You do not need to spend more than a few minutes to accomplish this. With practice each day, it will become an automatic response that will require very little effort. After you have spent some time memorizing the daily affirmation, continue to repeat it throughout the day. Use anything you want to remind yourself to say the affirmation. I have trained myself to repeat my mantra for the day every time I look at my watch. In this way, I begin to build the affirmation into my subconscious, setting myself up to react and succeed when I am confronted with circumstances of extreme stress.

It is important to note that under times of stress, our cognitive ability—the ability to process information and think—is severely limited due to hormonal heart-rate increases. Therefore, reaction without conscious thought, based on our training, is the goal we are seeking. For the true warrior, it is the only acceptable level to obtain. This is why it is so important to train not only our bodies, but our minds as well. Without complete training, we will not be nearly as efficient in reacting to a crisis. Each mantra will help you to reach this level of training and improve your reaction under extreme stress.

Each accompanying page has a series of quotes. These quotes are from people who have inspired others to seek greatness, to reach deep within. I chose the quotes in this book as words of encouragement, to provoke thought and to inspire the warrior spirit to burn within you. You will notice that some of the quotes will contradict one another. Get over it. Life is about dichotomy. Some quotes may not seem to belong to the mantra for the day . . . or do they? Don't complain, whine or otherwise try to overanalyze my choices, I want you to THINK! Most of us are content to be spoon-fed our information, relying on the expertise of others rather than thinking for ourselves. Don't take my word for anything. This book will give you a direct, tangible experience, and you will be able to see for yourself the positive changes it can have on your life. Think, think, think!

You will also find sprinkled throughout this book my thoughts, observations and personal experiences, as I comment on the various themes we will explore on this journey. These thoughts come from the extensive research I conducted in writing this book, my life experiences, and my eighteen years as a peace officer. My hope is to share with you the good, bad, and ugly aspects of my experiences as a warrior so we can all learn and grow.

Once you have finished the book, I would recommend that you start reading a mantra daily and repeat this process until the book's pages are dog-eared and worn through. The more you read the warrior affirmations in this book, the deeper you will ingrain them in your consciousness. This will directly and positively affect your ability to respond to a crisis situation. Consistent practice of these techniques will ensure you a steady progress and continuing development. Make a commitment to use this book everyday to enhance your ability to protect those that depend on you.

I have also included a notes section for your use at the end of this book. I would encourage you to write down any experiences, thoughts or discoveries you have on your journey. You may also want to use this section to develop additional mantras specific to your individual needs. At the end of this book you will be able to find information on my website. Please feel free to check my website for contact information and other related materials that may assist you in the development of your warrior skills.

You must realize the essence of a warrior is constantly to seek improvement. Hold yourself to the higher standard, and fully accept your chosen role in life. Embrace the principles and ideals that have guided so many brave souls before you in the path of a warrior, and never doubt the power of your soul to overcome any circumstance you will face.

*There is more in us than we know. If we can be made to see it, perhaps, for the rest of our lives, we will be unwilling to settle for less.*

—Kurt Hahn (1886–1974),
founder, Outward Bound

*It takes an instant to create a hero.*
*It takes a lifetime to create a warrior.*
*Evil has no place to hide when it is forced to dwell among heroes and warriors.*

—Phil Messina—Modern Warrior

# The Beginning

I will survive.

I will survive!

**I WILL SURVIVE!!**

# Shared Thoughts:
# Visualize Survival

*This is as true in everyday life as it is in battle: We are given one life, and the decision is ours whether to wait for circumstances to make up our mind, or whether to act, and in acting, to live.*

—Omar Bradley, U.S. general

*You ask, "What is our policy?" I will say: "It is to wage war, by sea, land and air, with all our might and with all the strength that God can give us, to wage war against a monstrous tyranny, never surpassed in the dark, lamentable catalogue of human crime. That is our policy." You ask, "What is our aim?" I can answer with one word: Victory—victory at all costs; victory in spite of all terror; victory, however long and hard the road may be; for without victory, there is no survival.*

—Sir Winston Churchill (1874–1965),
1940, in his first address as
British prime minister

As a warrior, your entire being must be wrapped around one key word, one key concept. This concept is survival. Survival at all costs! There are no other options. There are no other outcomes. There are no other possibilities. The one and only thought you should ever have is that of surviving every mission, no matter what may come, no matter how horrific the circumstance. Never, ever entertain failure—not even for an instant. To give in to thoughts of failure can literally mean the difference between life and death when you are in a survival situation. In our moments of weakness, when that dreaded thought, "I can't do this," creeps into our consciousness, we become vulnerable. As warriors we cannot allow this weak mental state to take over. It is, quite simply, unacceptable.

It is vital that you adopt a survival mentality now. Make this commitment to yourself right now, this instant, and never look back. Do not waste another moment visualizing yourself as anything but a survivor. See yourself in your mind's eye involved in critical situations, making good decisions, and surviving. Mentally challenge yourself with worst-case scenarios, and always see yourself being victorious. Make a commitment to say this key mantra, "I will survive!" every single day. Say it with absolute conviction. Say it with fire and determination. Say it with an ironclad and indomitable will. Say it for the rest of your life, and never accept anything less.

If you asked me to outline the most important concept of being a warrior, it is the survival attitude. I have seen people who possessed far less skill than an opponent they had to face, and yet they were able to defeat their opponent soundly in a fight because they possessed a superior mental attitude. They fought with the absolute belief they would prevail. They fought with their entire soul committed to surviving. Defeat never entered their minds, and so, even with lesser skills, they were victorious. I would venture that each of you can think of an example that you have witnessed in your life where this was so. I would bet a good deal of you were incredulous, hardly able to believe what you had seen. Believe it, it's real. This is the survival attitude I am talking about. How can you explain this in any other way?

So how can we cultivate a survival attitude? It is true that a chosen few are born with this frame of mind already firmly in place. I have met several people who, even as small children, exhibited this survival attitude as a character trait. However, most of us do not have a natural survival attitude instilled from birth. It is something we develop, cultivating it over time and through experience and training. We must struggle against the doubt from the shadows of our consciousness that limits us. It is this doubt that must be erased, driven from the darkness into the light, through the use of this powerful mantra: I will survive!

It is vital you understand that the mantras in this book are meaningless—useless—if they are not recited with conviction. This is an exercise that demands intense, focused concentration. Say each over and over. "I will survive. I will survive. I will survive!" Say it until you mean it. Don't go through the motions halfheartedly. This is a waste of your time. Dig deep, and say it like a warrior, from the depths of your soul. You can do this, you can succeed, and you **WILL** survive! With the right mental attitude, there can be no other outcome. Failure will be driven from you, crushed, and never allowed to haunt your consciousness again. I challenge you, here and now, to make up your mind and commit to this essential principle and embrace the life-altering power that is within you!

I will win.

I will win!

I will win!!

*Here is the answer which I will give to President Roosevelt . . . We shall not fail or falter; we shall not weaken or tire. Neither the sudden shock of battle nor the long-drawn trials of vigilance and exertion will wear us down. Give us the tools and we will finish the job.*

—Sir Winston Churchill,
radio speech, 1941

*Victorious warriors win first and then go to war, while defeated warriors go to war first and then seek to win.*
—Sun Tzu (~300 B.C.),
*The Art of War*, Strategic Assessments

I have succeeded in the face of danger before.

## I have succeeded in the face of danger before.

## I have succeeded in the face of danger before!

*Nothing average ever stood as a monument to progress. When progress is looking for a partner, it doesn't turn to those who believe they are only average. It turns instead to those who are forever searching and striving to become the best they possibly can. If we seek the average level, we cannot hope to achieve a high level of success. Our only hope is to avoid being a failure.*

—A. Lou Vickery, business author

*The world is a dangerous place to live, not because of the people who are evil, but because of the people who don't do anything about it.*

—Albert Einstein, physicist

I will not rush rashly into danger.

**I will not rush rashly into danger.**

**I will not rush rash-ly into danger!**

*Take calculated risks. That is quite different from being rash.*

—George S. Patton, U.S. general

**There is nothing wrong with escaping from combat if you are overpowered and honestly cannot win the fight.**

—Miyamoto Musashi—*Book of Five Rings*

*The policy of being too cautious is the greatest risk of all.*

—Jawaharlal Nehru,
Indian politician and statesman

*Risk—If one has to jump a stream and knows how wide it is, he will not jump. If he doesn't know how wide it is, he'll jump and six times out of ten, he'll make it.*

—Persian

# Shared Thoughts:
# Time is on your side!

When I started police work, I can tell you that slowing down and not rushing into danger was by far the most difficult concept for me to understand. Being in my twenties, feeling strong and invincible with the testosterone of youth, it was not uncommon for me to leap before I took a good look! I can tell you now that many times it was sheer luck I was not killed or seriously injured by my rash actions. I am grateful my youthful exuberance did not result in getting anyone else hurt or killed either—again mostly because of luck. I will share a short war story with you to emphasize my point.

I was on patrol in a high-crime area with my partner. We were riding in a flat-top car with no visible light bar, and I was in the passenger seat. As we drove around a corner, I observed a hand-to-hand drug deal going down. The dealer took one look at the car and bolted. Without thinking, I jumped out, ran past the person who was buying the drugs, and chased the dealer. I left my partner alone in the middle of a very hostile neighborhood to deal with a suspect who had not been controlled or searched.

While I was running in a full sprint, my portable radio

failed, making communication with my dispatcher and other officers impossible. This was not uncommon in my city. The radio system was old, and due to the hilly topography, radio communication was often difficult. I couldn't have cared less; all I wanted was the dealer. I continued to run, jumping fences, yelling for the dealer to stop, through a dangerous neighborhood. Never once did I consider that I could be running into an ambush. Never once did I worry about my partner. I was too caught up in the chase, with my ego fully engaged. The only thing I cared about was making the arrest.

Ultimately, I lost the dealer near a dark carport. I stopped, nearly breathless, physically spent, and started a slow search of the area with my gun out. Suddenly, out of nowhere, the dealer appeared from the carport and surrendered. I was dismayed that he simply gave up without a fight. If he had any idea of how exhausted I was, he might have tried a different strategy. I placed this low-level, dope-dealing transgressor in handcuffs, and walked him back to the patrol car with my chest stuck out with foolish pride all over my face. When I finally arrived at my car, a small army of officers were waiting, worried because I had not been heard from for several minutes. I assured them "Super Cop" was OK, and I went back to the carport to search for evidence.

I discovered a bag containing about twenty small rocks of crack cocaine. I also discovered, from the location of the bag that the dealer had been in a perfect place to watch me. How long had he been there, watching my every move? It was a perfect ambush situation, but the dealer chose to dump his dope and give up. Had he been of the mind-set to attack me, I was a perfect target. On that particular day he did not want to kill a cop. On that particular day, I did everything wrong, and I was damn lucky to escape the entire incident without being hurt. What was even more amazing, I received a commendation for the arrest! The praise I received simply reinforced a pattern of behavior that took me years to overcome.

I know now experiences that like the one I have just related occur every day in police work. I watch the new officers in my agency making the same mistakes I used to make. As a trainer, I use stories like this one to help reinforce the fact that rushing rashly into danger is a fool's choice. Sooner or later, rash decisions will catch up to you and make you pay a dear price.

I now know that in most instances we can control the pace at which events unfold. It is very rare that an instant reaction to an event is necessary. When those times occur, I know my training will carry the day to a successful conclusion. In all other circumstances, I know time is on my side. I use it to my advantage, making sure that tactically I have the upper hand. I know there are some who disagree with slowing things down. But I tell you this: Losing your life over a street-level drug dealer is unacceptable. If, as a warrior, I choose to sacrifice my life, you can damn sure bet it will not be spent in an unworthy cause.

I can control my fear at all times.

**I can control my fear at all times.**

**I can control my fear at all times!**

*Ah, this is obviously some strange usage of the word "safe" that I wasn't previously aware of.*

—Douglas Adams, Arthur Dent
in *The Hitchhiker's Guide to the Galaxy*

*I must not fear. Fear is the mind-killer. Fear is the little-death that brings total obliteration. I will face my fear. I will permit it to pass over me and through me. And when it has gone past I will turn the inner eye to see its path. Where the fear has gone there will be nothing. Only I will remain.*

—Frank Herbert, author of
the *Dune* science-fiction series

*You gain strength, courage and confidence by every experience in which you really stop to look fear in the face. You are able to say to yourself, "I have lived through this horror. I can take the next thing that comes along." You must do the thing you think you cannot do.*

—Eleanor Roosevelt,
American first lady

*Courage is resistance to fear, mastery of fear—not absence of fear.*

—Mark Twain, American author

*Cowards die many times before their deaths; The valiant never taste of death but once.*

—William Shakespeare, *Julius Caesar*,
Act II, Scene 2, line 32

# Shared Thoughts:
# Acknowledge Fear

The pressure on today's warriors in law enforcement and the military to be fearless is phenomenal. Popular media portray police officers as fighting Gods who can solve every problem they encounter in sixty minutes. It is the same for the military who are portrayed as able to handle anything laid in their path, leaving behind a wake of their enemies' bodies and scorched earth. Society demands fearlessness of those who have chosen the path of a warrior. This is simply the badge of courage a warrior must wear; never acknowledging the raw emotions that fear can bring. Stand tall no matter the cost! Even your peers, casting a shadow of suspicion on your ability to be trusted in a combat situation, often see acknowledging fear as a weakness. One thing is for sure: Anyone who tells you they are fearless is either a liar or a psychopath. The key is to understand and embrace your fear and then use it to your advantage. The first step toward this goal is acknowledging the existence of fear.

As a police officer, I have had to face many dangerous situations. Some of these situations were life threatening. Early in my career, when I did not understand the dynamics of my body's response to fear, I found myself overwhelmed to the point of inaction in the face of an extreme threat. However, over the years, as I learned to understand, accept and ultimately embrace my fear, I came to realize that I could also control it and use it to my advantage. Fear can be one of the greatest inspirations a person can receive when it is properly channeled. It may seem unusual to believe that something so negative could be turned into a positive. To help us understand this concept, let's take a look at the body's physiological response to fear and stress.

One of the greatest obstacles to controlling stress is our built-in physiological response. By now, we are all familiar with the fight-or-flight theory. The body, in preparing to face an extreme threat, causes our heart rate to increase with a flood of chemicals. It is a survival reflex ingrained from the beginning of man. This hormonally induced heart-rate increase can send our pulse up to extreme levels in seconds. Blood is pulled from our extremities, and we are no longer concerned with basic physiological functions. Once our heart rate climbs above 175 beats per minute, it is likely that we will experience the symptoms of fight or flight.

Common physiological responses to this fight-or-flight type of heart rate increase include: irrational freezing, voiding of bowel and bladder, panic fleeing, inability to react physically, and an inability to think and process information. The bottom line is this type of event can render you confused, dazed, and useless. Once you are overwhelmed, you may not be able to recover in time to engage your threat properly. This can obviously jeopardize the people you are trying to help. Worse, it can make you vulnerable, defenseless, and primed to become a victim. A situation that is unacceptable and, through proper training, avoidable.

Before we go any further, there is an important distinction that needs to be made between hormonally-induced heart-rate increases and exercise-induced heart-rate increases. The two are not related in the sense that they do not affect the body in the same way physiologically. Exercise-induced heart-rate increases do not have the flood of epinephrine, adrenaline, and other chemicals associated with a hormonal heart-rate increase. You control exercise heart-rate increases through the amount of effort and stress you consciously place on your body. Hormonal heart-rate increases are uncontrolled, largely unconscious responses to certain threatening events. Therefore, even if you exercise your heart rate to extreme levels, it will do very little to prepare you mentally for an event causing a hormonal heart-rate increase.

During a threatening event, your body dumps hormones into your bloodstream and you feel a surge, often referred to as an adrenaline pump. This should trigger a realization within you that you are now moving toward the optimum physiological range to deal with the threat. Yes, that rush we so often associate with fear is actually a good thing! As your heart rate rises, you will very quickly (within a few seconds) move into a hormonally induced heart-rate range of 115 to 145 beats per minute.

This is where you need to stay. At this range, only fine-motor skills, such as writing with a pen, deteriorate. Gross-motor skills, such as shooting a weapon, or punching and kicking, will still be available to you. In this range, you will still have the ability to think, focus and move. How well you do so will depend upon your level of training. Your body is primed, pumped and in the zone for combat. If you can maintain this range you will remain a formidable opponent, ready to deal with whatever threat faces you.

Now comes the big challenge: keeping your body from rising out of this zone while faced with an extreme threat. Going beyond the optimum 145 beats per minute will start you down the path toward losing your ability to respond to the threat. How can you keep yourself under control and in the combat zone? If your body's response to extreme stress is a built-in physiological response, it seems beyond your control to do anything about it. However, if you begin to train yourself to recognize this response, there is something you can do that is tremendously effective in helping to control your heart rate. Through a simple breathing technique, you can begin to take control of your fear.

This breathing technique has been referred to as autogenic breathing, or combat breathing. Here's how it works. When you are suddenly confronted with an event that causes an uncontrolled increase in your heart rate, or you are beginning a mission that you know in advance will be stressful, begin the following breathing technique:

- Take in a breath for a count of three.
- Hold the breath for a count of three.
- Release the breath for a count of three.
- Repeat as often as necessary.

You can repeat this cycle as long as necessary to reduce your heart rate and keep it under control. The more you train with this technique, the more effective it will become. I know police officers that have begun to train with this technique every chance they get and they are reporting excellent results in controlling their stress. I use this technique as often as possible. As a police officer, I have had to face danger every day I have worked on the street. I began using this technique every time I received a "hot" radio call.

As soon as the call came in, I started autogenic breathing. While driving to the call, with lights flashing and siren blaring, I continued the breathing until I reached the scene of the emergency and engaged whatever threat or challenge was waiting for me. I can tell you from personal experience, the effects of this technique are amazing. It immediately helps me to stay calm, centered and focused. Even during extreme events, I have been able to keep my composure with great success. Without a doubt, I have become a more effective warrior because of this simple technique.

The best way to practice this technique is in the field under stress conditions. However, to begin to understand the basics of autogenic breathing, try using this technique after intense exercise. As we discussed earlier, the exercise heart-rate increase is not the same. The technique will work to slow your heart rate. This will give you additional opportunities to practice the technique in a controlled environment. Any advance preparation you can make will help you when it comes time to apply it in a field situation.

As with any new training, you should practice daily, under any conditions that cause you stress. Before meetings, presentations, speaking engagements or any situation that causes your heart rate to increase, try this simple technique. The more you practice, the more this response will become automatic. Once mastered, you will be better able to control your body's physiological response to stress, allowing you to function at a higher level in the field.

Remember that the hardest step in learning to control your body's response to extreme stress is acknowledging it in the first place. Get past the stigma associated with embracing fear. Fear is real. If you do not acknowledge this natural physiological response, you are setting yourself up for failure. At some point, fear will consume and control you if you do not learn to embrace it. Take control, learn more about your body, and train yourself to respond in all situations. This is the path of a warrior, acknowledging what is perceived to be a weakness and turning it into strength. With very little effort, you will be able to transcend the negative effects of fear by becoming its master.

I will recognize danger and react
instantly.

# I will recognize danger
# and react instantly.

# I will recognize
# danger and react
# instantly!

*Carry the battle to them. Don't let them bring it to you. Put them on the defensive. And don't ever apologize for anything.*

—Harry S. Truman, thirty-third
president of the United States

*I have seen soldiers panic at the first sight of battle and a wounded squire pulling arrows out from his wound to fight and save his dying horse. Nobility is not a birthright, but is defined by one's action.*

—Kevin Costner, *Robin Hood,*
*Prince of Thieves,* 1991

*I know that every good and excellent thing in the world stands moment by moment on the razor-edge of danger and must be fought for . . .*

—Thornton Wilder, American playwright

# Shared Thoughts: Kicking Ass

I would like to talk briefly about a topic that causes the stomachs of most police administrators to bubble and churn like active volcanoes. That is the concept of reacting instantly and taking the fight to your opponent before they take it to you. The public in general has a difficult time understanding the true danger the modern warrior faces. This is especially true in the world of law enforcement.

Most administrators, long removed from the field, have forgotten how dangerous certain people and events can be. Most can acknowledge intellectually the challenges that a warrior faces, but that is where their depth of understanding seems to end. Their concerns are often more focused on pleasing their constituents and the public than on the safety of their front line personnel.

Many in the command structure have a difficult time relating to the honed skills that a warrior needs to perceive, react, and survive a threat. Often, they no longer understand warrior tactics, and in this kinder, gentler society, the thought of attacking your opponents before they can strike is seen as being too aggressive or too violent. However, when properly applied, taking the fight to your opponent before they attack is an essential edge to surviving a violent encounter. Waiting until someone decides to attack you is giving a huge advantage to your opponent and will reduce your chances of survival significantly. That is simply unacceptable.

Rules, laws, morals, and ethics do not hinder your opponent. You can damn sure bet focused, well-trained opponents will use your unwillingness to launch an attack to their advantage. They will wait for an opening, a sign of weakness or distraction, and launch an explosive assault against you. In the face of multiple opponents, the threat to your safety expands exponentially. Reacting in time to stop this kind of an attack is nearly impossible for all but the most advanced and prepared warrior. It therefore becomes crucial to recognize preattack indicators presented by your opponents and to take action before they can surprise you. When you decide to act, you must do so with complete conviction.

Preattack indicators can range from the obvious squaring off in a fighting stance to a subtle shoulder shift or target glance. Your perception may be as subtle as your intuitive sixth sense, a feeling that you are in danger. It is during this time that you must listen to that inner voice and take action before your opponent has the chance to launch an attack. It does not mean you have to do something as dramatic as smashing in his face, but it does mean you need to move in and take some kind of control. Even verbally challenging your opponent can be effective. Letting your opponent know you are aware of what he is trying to do can be very disarming. This may cause your opponent to rethink his pending attack against you. Whatever you decide to do, don't wait for the attack to come to you. Take the attack to him when you are legally and morally justified.

I know there is more than one option
to resolve all circumstances.

# I know there is more than one option to resolve all circumstances.

# I know there is more than one option to resolve all circumstances!

*In preparing for battle, I have always found that plans are useless, but planning is indispensable.*
> —Dwight D. Eisenhower, U.S. general
> and thirty-fourth president of the United States

*The best victory is when the opponent surrenders of its own accord before there are any actual hostilities . . . It is best to win without fighting.*
> —Sun Tzu (~300 B.C.), *The Art of War,*
> Planning a Siege

*The shaft of the arrow had been feathered with one of the eagle's own plumes. We often give our enemies the means of our own destruction.*
> —Aesop (~550 B.C.),
> "The Eagle and the Arrow"

# *Shared Thoughts:*
# *Visualize Victory*

---

We tend to make ourselves crazy with planning. Planning, planning, and more planning. All this planning often leads to a form of action that has missed the mark and is completely useless. However, mental preparation is essential, especially when we are responding with limited information to an incident that is unfolding quickly. If you are not familiar with the concept of mental crisis rehearsal, you should be. As a peace officer, I often find myself responding to emergency calls for service with very little information. Trying to make a plan does not always work because I never had enough information in the first place, and events often change too quickly. However, imagining the worst-case scenario while heading to the call is an excellent way to prepare mentally for whatever may come.

The next time you are heading to an event requiring your attention as a warrior, visualize the worst thing that could happen. For example, let's say I am responding to some unknown disturbance at a residence. My initial preparation will address where I will stop my vehicle to approach the problem. If I pull up in front of the house, I could be setting myself up for a sniper assault. What would I do if I were suddenly fired upon as I arrived on the scene? Am I prepared to back out of the area? Do I have an exit route? Are there sources of cover available to me? Is the call in a hostile neighborhood?

Are you getting the picture? You are playing a "what if" series of thoughts in your mind. Paranoid? Hardly. This is good mental preparation. Remember, you have chosen to be a warrior. Therefore it is on you to prepare properly. It will help you overcome a significant threat because you will be ready for action. Anything less can catch you off guard, and the precious time you will waste in trying to figure out what to do and how to react can get you in serious trouble.

One last thought. For those of you who have a difficult time visualizing, I'm here to tell you this skill is NOT a gift. It is an acquired skill that each of us possesses, and it is limitless in how far you can develop it. You can train yourself in the art of visualization just as anything else you have ever trained for. Practice each and every time you find yourself responding to a threat, and you will hone this important skill in very little time. It can be a powerful force in your ongoing development as a warrior.

I will maintain my equipment in prop-er working order and train with it until I have achieved mastery!

*If you are going to die in battle then you should do so with the utmost respectability and dignity. It is a terrible shame to die in battle with your sword undrawn or yourself unable to use it correctly.*

—Miyamoto Musashi—*Book of Five Rings*

*You must constantly practice all of your techniques until they become second nature. Once they are part of your nature you can cease to think about them.*

—Miyamoto Musashi—*Book of Five Rings*

# Shared Thoughts: Train, Train, Train!

If you want to touch on one subject that truly drives my passion, congratulations, you have arrived at it. Yes, I'm about to embark on a lecture. I'm going to stand on a soapbox and preach the gospel of training because I feel it is the one area where we can always strive to make improvements. It is also the one area where we often do not put in the kind of effort we should. There are so many reasons, so many excuses to skip training. As a training manager for a police department, I have heard it all. There is nothing you could tell me, nothing that would surprise me in this regard.

Oh, in case you're wondering about the old "glass house theory," I find myself from time to time coming up with the same lame excuses to justify missing my own training. This is normal. We have lives outside our role as warriors. Family obligations, work commitments, chores, and on and on and on. So many things demand our time. But I tell you this: It is all a matter of setting your priorities and not allowing people to steal your time in wasted pursuits. This does not mean you cannot balance your other commitments in life. It means you build training into your life as a priority that ranks at the top, not the bottom, of your list.

I am constantly engaged in finding new and creative ways to keep my passion stoked so I can continue to train with proper intensity. My martial art training has taught me that there is no true level of total mastery in any art. Total mastery seems always to be just beyond one's reach. To me, this is the greatest of life's challenges. If total mastery were so easy to obtain, then we would quickly lose the desire and focus to reach our ultimate goals. Because training can always take us to new levels, I find it provides me with the ultimate motivation to continue to try to improve.

Training to your highest level can give you a huge advantage over your opponent. When you can react without conscious thought, you will become a very effective warrior. Imagine yourself being able to block a punch that was thrown by your opponent without even thinking about it. Pure, raw reaction is a powerful force. It feels amazing to move when you need to, and it justifies all the long hours spent training for that one moment when it all pays off. When you enjoy this feeling just once, I can guarantee training will become your top priority. The key is finding your personal motivation. Don't wait to get your ass kicked before you decide training is important. That kind of mentality has no place on the path of a warrior.

What is your personal motivation? How about because you owe it to your partner to be there for him when he needs your help? How about so you can go home, safe and healthy to the people who love you the most? How about because society needs your skills and bravery so they can sleep in peace and safety each night? How about the oath you swore to uphold when you became a warrior? How about for your own personal self-esteem? Find your motivation. Train constantly to the best of your abilities. Make your training intense and as close to real life as possible. Make the time, and never stop training. Above all, stop making excuses!

I will stay focused on my mission and complete my assignment.

I will stay focused on my mission and complete my assignment.

I will stay focused on my mission and complete my assignment!

*A mind troubled by doubt cannot focus on the course to victory.*

> —Arthur Golden,
> *Memoirs of a Geisha*

*It is wise to direct your anger towards problems—not people; to focus your energies on answers—not excuses.*

> —William Arthur Ward,
> author, editor, pastor

*Finish each day and be done with it. You have done what you could; some blunders and absurdities have crept in; forget them as soon as you can. Tomorrow is a new day; you shall begin it serenely and with too high a spirit to be encumbered with your old nonsense.*

> —Ralph Waldo Emerson,
> American essayist and poet

# Shared Thoughts: Focus People, Focus!

"All units be advised, car jacking just occurred." This is how my shift started one afternoon. It was about five in the afternoon when the call came in about a carjacking that had occurred in one of our local malls. The carjackers, a man and woman on a Bonnie-and-Clyde crime spree, had taken a large Ford long-bed pickup with a huge camper shell from the victim. In my particular city, there were two main freeways cutting the town into quadrants. I got onto a freeway on-ramp in my really, really fast Ford LTD and waited. Sure enough, within five minutes I spotted the pickup and pulled in behind.

"Central, I'm behind the stolen pickup. I'm in pursuit!"

As soon as I had pulled in behind the pickup, we were off. Actually, it was pretty sad. The huge pickup, with an oversized camper shell, was no match for my powerful patrol car. I easily kept pace as the pickup reached a maximum cruising speed of about 80-mph. Then the driver did something that took me a bit by surprise. Our initial direction was out of town, across a major bridge, and away from the congestion of the city and the other officers. Instead of just trying to lose me, the driver took an off-ramp and turned back toward the center of town on a frontage road. As we turned back toward town, the five o'clock rush hour was flooding the streets with people trying to get home, making conditions extremely dangerous. A second officer had joined the pursuit, so at least I had one person for backup, which helped to ease my mind a bit.

"Central, we are heading . . ."

At this point in the pursuit, our infamous* radio system crashed. This was a great radio system as long as an emergency did not exist. I swear that damn thing knew when the shit was hitting the fan and would simply melt down. This happened so often it was considered "normal"! I would have loved to get my hands on the propeller head that put our radio system together, but at that moment I had to stay focused. It was time to make a decision.

I was pursuing two dangerous criminals. Department policy stated that should the radio, lights, or siren fail at any time, the pursuit should be terminated. There I was with an angel cop on one shoulder telling me to back off and a devil cop on the other telling me to chase. Then I saw an amazing thing. The truck took a sharp turn and went up on two wheels. I have to tell you, it was an incredible thing to see. This huge truck, on two wheels, like something out of a movie, was just bizarre. The truck came crashing back down on all fours, and we proceeded toward a major intersection. The driver of the truck started pulling into the opposite lane of traffic, and was attempting to ram cars off the road in an effort to make me crash. That was it. My mind was made up. This guy was not going to get away.

My focus became laser sharp. Although this pursuit happened more than fifteen years ago, I can still remember every detail. The next thing that happened was nothing short of a miracle. The truck entered one of our busiest intersections at the peak of commute hour. I cringed at what I anticipated would be a major wreck, however, the driver was able to make an incredible right turn, literally threading the truck through the eye of a needle, going up on two wheels again and making it through the intersection without hitting anything. I was not so lucky.

I was so shocked that this guy made it, I lost my focus. Damn! I shot for the same hole in the traffic, but I was carrying too much speed. I drifted through the turn, nearly hit several cars, and slammed into the side of a cement median. The impact was significant, but the car kept rolling, so I stayed with it. I was pretty sure I caused some damage to the car because I was now holding onto a steering wheel that was shaking so badly I looked like I was a paint can getting mixed at the hardware store. The other clue was the smoke coming off the left side of my car. With my focus regained, I listened to Devil Cop and stayed in the pursuit.

Two more turns with the truck on two wheels. My car was now literally vibrating parts off it, me behind the wheel focused on hanging in to the bitter end. It was not a pretty picture. Just as my car was about to give up, the truck took its last turn. The driver pulled sharply into a driveway to a large parking lot at a strip mall. The truck heaved right, compressed the springs, and then violently shifted to the left. The truck went up on two wheels and cart-wheeled end over end on top of parked cars. After several rolls, and what would later be a field day for several insurance companies, the truck came to a sudden and violent halt on its side. Good news sir, we got your truck back!

I tried to stop. I really tried. However, my car was now devoid of brakes. Well, I quickly adapted to the situation and jammed the car into park. Yep, that did it. The car stopped, forever, right behind the truck. My left front tire was on fire—friction has a funny way of doing that—and the bad guys were still in the truck. Focus people, focus!

I got my shotgun out and much to my surprise Bonnie and Clyde were able to get out of the truck and surrender without any injuries whatsoever! It's always that way, isn't it? The bad guys survive the most amazing hell possible with only a scratch. Didn't seem quite fair somehow. I had a lot to deal with: reams of paperwork, an internal affairs investigation for policy violations, several dissatisfied members of the community, a serious adrenaline dump, a burning patrol car, and the now ever-present news media.

Now, how's that for an example of staying focused? I know. Stupid rookie. Bad cop, no doughnut. But let's get to the real lesson. No matter what event you find yourself engaged in as a warrior, you must stay completely focused on the task at hand. A momentary loss of focus can be disastrous. I can hear my friend, Mike Gray, right now. Mike had a saying he would always use when he sensed his students were drifting. "Focus people, focus!" Mike was right!

I will have a positive attitude.

# I will have a positive attitude.

# I will have a positive attitude!

*Weakness of attitude becomes weakness of character.*
—Albert Einstein, physicist

*Ability is what you're capable of doing. Motivation determines what you do. Attitude determines how well you do it.*
—Lou Holtz, football coach

*There are no menial jobs, only menial attitudes.*
—William Bennett, politician

*The greatest discovery of any generation is that a human being can alter his life by altering his attitude.*
—William James, American author

*We who lived in concentration camps can remember the men who walked through the huts comforting others, giving away their last piece of bread. They may have been few in number, but they offer sufficient proof that everything can be taken from a man but one thing: the last of human freedoms—to choose one's attitude in any given set of circumstances—to choose one's own way.*
—Victor Frank, author

# Shared Thoughts: Positive Attitude

The eternal question: "Is the glass half empty or half full?" I hate to bring up this overused metaphor for how one sees life, but its simple elegance makes the point beautifully. What kind of person are you? How do you see your glass? How do you react before, during, and after an extreme event?

I must tell you that I find myself constantly struggling with keeping a positive attitude. I have friends who can take the most negative events and find a ray of sunshine. I admire these friends. They are great warriors. These are men and women who have never lost their perspective. They reside in a faith so deep it is simply unshakable. They are among the strongest people I know, and though the world may be crashing down around them they are still able to stand in peace and confidence. Their positive attitude is absolutely contagious!

I have noticed one characteristic about people who are constantly able to keep a positive attitude. Each and every one of them is very introspective. They all spend a significant amount of time analyzing each event and their response to it. They do not take this analysis to the point of obsession, constantly beating themselves up over what could have been done differently. Rather, they look at an event from the perspective of what they can learn before moving on. The worst event simply means picking yourself up, dusting yourself off, realizing what went wrong, and learning how to avoid the problem in the future. They take each event as a chance for personal growth and learning. Most importantly, they acknowledge they are human and are at peace with the truth that we cannot always be right.

In the last few years, I have been making a sincere effort to apply the power of positive thinking to my life. I will admit I have not been completely successful. I still find myself slipping into a negative attitude from time to time when I am overwhelmed or fatigued. However, I can tell you that I have also made some significant improvements in this area and it feels great! When I can keep a positive perspective, events just seem to flow better. My ability to perform on my job is always improved when I approach the day with a positive attitude. After each call for service, I now find myself looking for any lessons I can learn. I'm getting better at keeping a positive attitude, and with a little effort you can too!

I will use deadly force in the defense of life.

# I will use deadly force in the defense of life.

# I will use deadly force in the defense of life!

*When you have the enemy in an awkward position, do not let him regain his composure and possibly defeat you. When the enemy is confused, you must go in for the kill.*

—Miyamoto Musashi—*Book of Five Rings*

*Any community's arm of force—military, police, security—needs people in it who can do necessary evil, and yet not be made evil by it. To do only the necessary and no more. To constantly question the assumptions, to stop the slide into atrocity.*

—Lois McMaster Bujold,
*Barrayar,* 1991

*Being a predator isn't always comfortable but the only other option is to be prey. That is not an acceptable option.*

—Phil Messina—Modern Warrior

*We did not ask for this mission, but we will fulfill it.*

—George W. Bush, forty-third
president of the United States

# *Shared Thoughts: Deadly Force*

I have one question for you. Have you really prepared yourself to use deadly force?

Answer this question honestly. I would be willing to bet that most of us have not fully embraced this potentially life-altering aspect of our role as warriors. Sure, we will swear an oath to uphold the Constitution. We will tell recruiters and job interviewers we are willing to resort to the ultimate use of force in the proper situations. But how much of that is just lip service? Are you just saying what people want to hear? Are you truly ready? Or, are you just hoping that when the time comes you will be able just to "react" and use deadly force? Worse yet, are you just hoping that you will never have to use deadly force, never acknowledging this potential reality?

This is not a matter of lusting for the kill. I'm not talking about becoming some wild-eyed, frothing, foam-at-the-mouth psychopath who just can't wait to spill some blood. This is about accepting the reality that you may, at a moment's notice, need to resort to deadly force to protect your life of the life of another. Have you truly prepared yourself? How often do you think about it? How often do you train for it? The truth is, if we are honest with ourselves, most of us have not adequately prepared. This lack of preparation can lead to hesitation or underreaction at a time when you must be instantly decisive and committed to your action.

Stop for a moment. Put this book down right now, and think about what I have said. Analyze yourself, find your weakness, and take steps, right now, to address any weakness you discover from your personal assessment. The role of the warrior can be serious business. We don't have the luxury of working on this aspect of being a warrior after the fact. Too much depends on what you have done to prepare now. What you are doing to prepare right now. Please, take some time to do some soul-searching, and make an honest evaluation of yourself. I will tell you this: You will not regret the time you spent working on this when the day comes for you to use deadly force.

I will not fear death.

**I will not fear death.**

**I will not fear death!**

*Generally speaking, the way of the warrior is resolute acceptance of death.*

—Miyamoto Musashi, 1645

*The true warrior doesn't seek war, nor does he wish to do battle. He merely believes that it is honorable to cling to a worthy cause. It is noble to reach out to those who are weaker than yourself. And it is valiant to believe that many things are worth giving up everything for.*

—Phil Messina—Modern Warrior

*It is not unseemly for a man to die fighting in defense of his country.*

—Homer (700 B.C.), *The Iliad*

*Let every nation know, whether it wishes us well or ill, we shall pay any price, bare any burden, meet any hardship, support any friend, oppose any foe, to assure the survival and success of liberty.*

—John F. Kennedy, thirty-fifth president of the United States

*Greater love has no man than this: That he give his life for his friends.*

—John 15:13

# Shared Thoughts:
# I Don't Want to Die!

I do not have a death wish. I do not approach my role as a warrior with the attitude of committing suicide, an act that would render all my years of training and service useless. If someone shoots at me, I can damn well guarantee you, I won't be calmly walking down the street like Dirty Harry, eating a hot dog, and annihilating everything in my path. "Feel lucky today, punk?"

No, I will be finding cover ASAP and using good tactics before I engage that kind of threat! Wasting your life does not make good sense. This type of action is often portrayed as being heroic, but I would argue it is foolish and goes directly against the path a warrior should travel. I was not put on this earth to sacrifice myself needlessly in the pursuit of a futile effort. However, I acknowledge and accept that my role as a warrior may cause me to lose my life in the pursuit of my duty. This seeming contradiction is part of the dichotomy of being a warrior. It is the nature of the job.

I know many warriors who have told me they would not risk their lives for anyone. There are a variety of reasons for making statements like this. I have heard my fellow warriors utter these words, and then on the very next call for service, I have seen them take action that placed them in lethal danger, without thought or hesitation, for someone they did not even know. Do you see the beauty of this reaction? They were not making suicidal moves. They were calculated actions based on proper training with a high likelihood of success. However, in taking this action, they placed themselves in a potentially deadly situation. They were, in effect, willing to risk their lives. Why?

I believe it is because taking this type of selfless action is ingrained in the warrior spirit. It is a part of the essence that defines who and what we are. We allow this spirit to control our actions because it is what we do best. The warrior spirit simply kicks in and we react, seemingly without conscious thought. It is our instinct, our essence, and it is a most precious gift. It is what separates us from the gentle souls we protect.

I also know many warriors who are not afraid to die. Their reasons for not fearing death are amazingly diverse. Some people are just devoid of the fear of death, but they cannot define exactly why. They are not reckless, but rather they exude a confidence in being able to overcome all circumstances without the conscious thought of death. Others take courage in having a strong faith in God and what awaits them after this life. Some, quite frankly, are just too stupid to realize they have placed themselves in a potentially lethal situation, while others just rely on plain old luck. The varied reasons for not fearing death are not really important. What is important is that as warriors, we do not let a fear of death hinder our ability to take action and that our actions are based on sound tactics and training.

As I stated at the beginning, I don't want to die, but I accept that death is possible in my role as a warrior. In the end, it comes down to the simple, resolute acceptance of death. As odd as it sounds, it is a part of becoming a warrior. Acceptance of death helps to define our unique role. It is not right or wrong, it just is. It is a real possibility, it is a part of the job, and it is an essential element in defining who we are.

I will overcome any threat with courage.

I will overcome any threat with courage.

I will overcome any threat with courage!

*Courage in danger is half the battle.*
> —Titus Maccius Plautus,
> Roman playwright

*A timid person is frightened before danger, a coward during the time, and a courageous person afterward.*
> —Jean Paul Richter,
> German author

*Courage is being scared to death—but saddling up anyway.*
> —John Wayne,
> American actor

*Above all things, never be afraid. The enemy who forces you to retreat is himself afraid of you at that very moment.*
> —André Maurois, French biographer,
> novelist, essayist

I will know my enemy.

I will know my enemy.

I will know my
enemy!

*Knowing is half the battle.*

—GI Joe

*If you know the enemy and know yourself, you need not fear the result of a hundred battles. If you know yourself but not the enemy, for every victory gained you will also suffer a defeat. If you know neither the enemy nor yourself, you will succumb in every battle.*

—Sun Tzu (~300 B.C.)

I will breathe deeply to control my
stress and tension.

# I will breathe deeply to control my stress and tension.

# I will breathe deeply to control my stress and tension!

*All things are ready if our minds be so.*

—U.S. Bureau of Alcohol,
Tobacco and Firearms video

*Breath control is the one channel that connects the body and the mind together. With this unity of body and mind comes the ability to control all things. Master proper, calm, autogenic breathing techniques and you will master stress and tension during crisis.*

—Rodger Ruge

I will *never* wait for an assailant to end my fight, even if it is with my last dying breath, I will always fight to win.

I will *never* wait for an assailant to end my fight, even if it is with my last dying breath, I will always fight to win.

I will *never* wait for an assailant to end my fight, even if it is with my last dying breath, I will always fight to win!

*The harder the conflict, the more glorious the triumph. What we obtain too cheap, we esteem too lightly; it is the dearness only that gives everything its value. I love the man that can smile in trouble, that can gather strength from distress and grow brave by reflection. 'Tis the business of little minds to shrink; but he whose heart is firm, and whose conscience approves his conduct, will pursue his principles unto death.*

—Thomas Paine, American Revolution
pamphleteer, patriot

*Far better it is to dare mighty things, to win glorious triumphs even though checkered by failure, than to rank with those poor spirits who neither enjoy nor suffer much because they live in the gray twilight that knows neither victory nor defeat.*

—Theodore Roosevelt, twenty-sixth
president of the United States

# Shared Thoughts: Never, Ever Give Up!

Remember the Black Knight character in the Monty Python movie, *The Holy Grail*? Remember how after the Black Knight has been hacked to pieces, literally having his arms and legs removed by his opponent, he mockingly taunts his assailant as he is riding off, bantering at him to come back because he can still bite him! Ludicrous and absurd, but as crazy as that movie is, that's the right attitude for a warrior. Indeed, we all need to be like the Black Knight, never willing to give up.

I have seen people so badly damaged from car accidents, shootings, and stabbings that there was no doubt in my mind they would succumb to their wounds. Yet, remarkably, they survived. Why? How? In other situations, I have seen people with relatively minor injuries die before they even made it to the hospital. These people should have survived! Again, the questions of why and how beg to be asked. It has been my personal observation, time and time again, that there is one key difference between the people who lived and the people who died. Very simply, it boiled down to the attitude of never giving up.

The people who survived fought hard to live. Their passion for survival was resolute. Often, they came from backgrounds of struggle and turmoil. Constantly bathed in conditions that were harsh, they would struggle for survival every day. Therefore, it comes as no surprise that they were tougher and had a mind-set that was programmed to overcome anything set in their path. These people were strong, focused, and unwilling to give up.

Many of those who died were not strong people, either mentally or physically. They had never seen or been exposed to situations that placed their lives in danger. Many came from lives of comfort and wealth. I would be willing to bet they had never been seriously challenged at any point during their lives. They did not possess the passion to survive, and when life tested them, they were not ready for the challenge. Are you?

As warriors, if we are placed in a situation demanding we fight for our lives, we must be willing to fight to the last possible moment. We must never give up, even when all hope seems lost. Indeed, it is often at that moment of seeming hopelessness that the true essence of our nature bursts forth to overcome insurmountable obstacles. We can do the "impossible," we can overcome amazing circumstances and stand victorious. Do you believe?

I tell you that you must believe, with all your heart. You must cultivate this attitude of survival, of never giving up. You must have an enduring attitude of faith in yourself and your skills. You must recognize the worthiness in fighting to the bitter end. When you can do this, you will have become a complete warrior and a formidable force to be reckoned with. Evil will have no choice but to hide when faced with such a force. It will cower in the shadows knowing what awaits it.

Believe!

I accept my chosen role as a warrior.

## I accept my chosen role as a warrior.

## I accept my chosen role as a warrior!

*Every man has his own destiny: the only imperative is to follow it, to accept it, no matter where it leads him.*

—Henry Miller, American author

*And when man faces destiny, destiny ends and man comes into his own.*

—Andre Malraux, French author
and resistance leader

*We cannot change anything until we accept it. Condemnation does not liberate, it oppresses.*

—C. G. Jung, Swiss psychiatrist

*Advance, and never halt, for advancing is perfection. Advance and do not fear the thorns in the path, for they draw only corrupt blood.*

—Kahlil Gibran, poet, philosopher

# *Shared Thoughts:*
# *Acceptance*

Life is about self-discovery. The paths we choose, the experiences that shape and mold our future, all lead us ultimately to define who and what we are. We hope this process is a constant evolution with limitless growth—that we are challenging ourselves, pushing to achieve higher and higher levels of personal growth.

What is your grandest vision of yourself as a warrior? Have you fully accepted your chosen role?

For some, the role of warrior seems preordained from birth. You know the type of people I am talking about, those few who are always looked to for leadership and guidance in times of crisis. From early childhood, it was obvious where their paths would lead. For them, the role of warrior is second nature, completely natural. They flow like water around any resistance, seemingly guided by some force beyond our understanding. Why is this so for some and not so for others?

It has been my observation that one thing holds us back from becoming the best at what we choose. This one thing is not limited to the role of warrior. It applies to whatever we have chosen for ourselves in this lifetime. This concept is remarkably simple in context and incredibly difficult in application. It boils down to one word: acceptance. Complete and total acceptance of our grandest vision of who and what we wish to become.

Acceptance of ourselves as warriors means that we understand only a chosen few can fulfill this role. It means embracing our role as warrior and allowing it to define who and what we are. It is not a matter of pride or any other ego-based delusion. This is not about sticking your nose up in the air and feeling superior to others. It is about humble service. It is about being a sheepdog, keeping the wolves at bay and watching over the flock. It is about understanding that you possess special gifts that can help others. It is about accepting your destiny and always striving to improve your skills.

I will tell you that I was not a natural-born warrior. In fact, I have had significant struggles and many failures in trying to become the best warrior I can possibly be. Nothing I have achieved as a warrior has come easily. I had to work harder than most throughout my career because I was lacking the one element I needed to move beyond my self-induced limitations. Those limitations were manifested in a belief that I was not worthy to fulfill the role of a warrior. It has taken me many years of struggle and introspection to overcome this final obstacle. However, once I was able to accept my chosen role, things changed dramatically.

Acceptance boosted my self-confidence. With this acceptance, I experienced a large growth in my abilities. I was able to cast aside feelings of inadequacy and an ego shrouded in fear with simple acceptance. I have accepted my skills, my abilities, and most importantly, my limitations. I have accepted my choice to become a warrior. I have accepted my self-worth in serving my fellow citizens. I believe in myself. This core principle of acceptance is what helped me close the circle. I have now truly accepted my role and I delight in the comfort of knowing it was the right choice. This will happen for you as well. Constantly move toward this goal until you, too, can feel the inner peace of acceptance.

I will see myself victorious in all actions.

# I will see myself victorious in all actions.

# I will see myself victorious in all actions!

*Of every 100 men:*
- *Ten should not even be here*
- *Eighty are nothing but targets*
- *Ten are real fighters*

*We are lucky to have them . . . they the battle make.*

        —Hericletus, 500 B.C., philosopher

*We must become the change we want to see.*

        —Mahatma Gandhi, Indian nationalist,
        pacifist, social reformer

*The true warrior lives a life of contradiction for he strives to create a world in which he is no longer needed.*

        —Phil Messina—Modern Warrior

I know the proper tactics I need to win.

I know the proper tactics I need to win.

I know the proper tactics I need to win!

*Excellence is not a single act, but a habit.*

—Aristotle, ancient
Greek philosopher

*Training, to be of any value, must be constant and challenging. You must train with all your heart and soul, seeking with every new challenge new personal improvement. It is not a matter of becoming as good as this person or as good as that person . . . it is a matter of becoming the best that you can be. It is not enough to muddle through your training; you must give everything you have, combined with total concentration and complete intensity. Proper practice can even overcome a lack of natural talent if you are willing to work hard enough. When you can accomplish your mission through pure reaction then you have achieved true mastery through your training. This should always be your goal whenever you train . . . total mastery!*

—Rodger Ruge

*Smooth seas do not make a skillful sailor.*

—African proverb

I can face and overcome any threat.

## I can face and over-come any threat.

# I can face and over-come any threat!

*We're a peaceful nation. Yet, as we have learned, so suddenly and so tragically, there can be no peace in a world of sudden terror. In the face of today's new threat, the only way to pursue peace is to pursue those who threaten it.*

—George W. Bush, forty-third
president of the United States

*One ought never to turn one's back on a threatened danger and try to run away from it. If you do that, you will double the danger. But if you meet it promptly and without flinching, you will reduce the danger by half.*

—Sir Winston Churchill (1874-1965),
British prime minister

I will seek a peaceful resolution
whenever possible.

# I will seek a peaceful resolution whenever possible.

# I will seek a peaceful resolution whenever possible!

*Every kind of peaceful cooperation among men is primarily based on mutual trust and only secondarily on institutions such as courts of justice and police.*
—Albert Einstein, physicist

*To fight and conquer in all your battles is not supreme excellence; supreme excellence consists in breaking the enemy's resistance without fighting.*
—Sun Tzu (~300 B.C.)

# Shared Thoughts:
# Seek Peace

There was a time in my career where I met every challenge with force. It did not matter to me that there were other options at my disposal that required less effort and risk. My persona as a young police officer was to be aggressive and confrontational. I had to prove to my peers that I could handle myself, and the pressure to perform was tremendous. Everyone was watching the new guy, and I believed I had to act this way in order to gain the respect of my peers, the citizens I served, and the bad guys I confronted daily. Anything less, I believed, was perceived as a weakness.

I was expected to be the kind of person who could be counted on when the shit really hit the fan. Don't get me wrong, this is definitely an important component of being a police officer. Being ready, willing, and able to apply force is absolutely a necessary part of the job. I would never suggest anything less. The problem was, I started to let this aggressive, badge-heavy, rookie mentality completely consume me. I started to turn into a street monster, and I started to slide.

In order to back up this attitude, I began to train constantly, obsessively. I exercised daily and used weights to increase my strength. I studied and practiced my defensive-tactics skills and applied them as often as possible in the field. Each day, with each new success, I grew more confident, aggressive, arrogant, and quite frankly, dangerous. I was over-confident. The fact that there were people I might have to face who were bigger, badder, and didn't have anything to lose never entered my mind. I was a veteran officer's night-mare. I would often jack up a suspect that a veteran officer had kept calm, and this would result in a fight that did not need to take place. I was heading toward being out of control, and I was primed to get my ass kicked.

Then a remarkable thing happened. When I first started the job, another officer who had been with the department for about eighteen months befriended me. His name is Ralph Pata. We quickly developed a friendship and trust that was rooted in the shared experiences of police work. We worked several shift rotations together, and were always beat partners. Out of all the people in our department, I trusted his opinion and judgment the most. As I started to transform into the street monster I described above, Ralph was watching. When I was at my worst, Ralph pulled me aside and, with complete sincerity and respect, he did what only a good and trusted friend can do. He told me to pull my head out of my ass.

I was stunned! Rocked to the core. It was the proverbial slap across the face that I needed. Ralph jarred me out of my ego-drenched stupor and helped me to discover another part of myself that was waiting to emerge. Through Ralph, I was able to realize it was actually OK to resolve disputes without resorting to force and still keep the respect of my peers, the citizens, and even the bad guys. Oh yeah, I still find myself in situations where force needs to be applied. But, ever since that day, I have been able to develop my verbal skills to resolve most things peacefully. The result has been phenomenal. My peers, the community, and even those people who find themselves on the wrong side of the law respect me for my ability to keep the peace. It is amazing how simple respect, patience, and the willingness to allow another to save face can result in a peaceful resolution.

Know what drives me crazy now? That's right, rookies who were just like me!

My will is ironclad and indomitable,
I will never know defeat.

My will is ironclad and indomitable, I will never know defeat.

My will is ironclad and indomitable, I will never know defeat!

*All of the significant battles are waged within the self.*
—Sheldon Kopp,
American psychologist

*We will not waiver; we will not tire; we will not falter;
we will not fail. Peace and freedom will prevail.*
—George W. Bush, forty-third
president of the United States

I will hold myself to the highest standard of ethics and values.

## I will hold myself to the highest standard of ethics and values.

## I will hold myself to the highest standard of ethics and values!

*True courage is not the brutal force of vulgar heroes, but the firm resolve of virtue and reason.*

—Alfred North Whitehead,
British mathematician,
logician, and philosopher

*The art of being yourself at your best is the art of unfolding your personality into the person you want to be. . . . Be gentle with yourself, learn to love yourself, to forgive yourself, for only as we have the right attitude toward ourselves can we have the right attitude toward others.*

—Wilfred Peterson,
"This Week" (Oct. 1, 1961)

*Character cannot be developed in ease and quiet. Only through experience of trial and suffering can the soul be strengthened, ambition inspired, and success achieved.*

—Helen Keller, blind American
lecturer and author

# Shared Thoughts:
# Hold Your Head High

Ethical struggles. How do we define what is right and wrong? If I think something is wrong, and you think something is right, who is correct? What is proper ethical conduct in one culture is improper in another. Yet, in the context of each culture, these conflicting ethical definitions are correct. Mankind has struggled with the concept of right and wrong forever. The very nature of right and wrong has changed over the years and continues to evolve as time marches on. So, as warriors, where do we draw our ethical lines? What standards do we hold ourselves to when ethical boundaries of right and wrong can be separated by the width of a razor's edge?

Allow me to impart a war story regarding the concept of right and wrong. A long time ago, in a very unique part of California, I was working as a patrol officer when I received a call regarding a rabid rat. Mr. Rat was apparently causing significant concern for several patrons of a local Macy's, who were standing outside the store waiting for the doors to open. When I arrived on the scene, there were about twenty amused people ready to watch the show and one greasy, shaking, slimy, frothing-at-the-mouth rat.

This was no ordinary rat. This was a rather large wharf rat that would give a cat a run for its money in a fight. I immediately called for animal control and got out of my car to try and contain the rat. (Stupid rookie!) I used my baton to keep the rat trapped in a corner of the building. However, every time I got close to the rat it would rear up, and, I kid you not, growl! I have to tell you, I was not happy about dealing with this rat. To make matters a bit more stressful, the crowd had now grown to about thirty bantering people.

After a few minutes of playing rodeo rat, a well-meaning lady came over and handed me a box. She gently suggested that I use the box to trap the rat and thus solve my dilemma. Great idea lady! Did I mention the box was only slightly larger than the rat?

Lacking any other options, I decided to do a stupid thing and trap the rat. Now, I know what a majority of you are thinking right now. You want to know why I did not use my baton to club that rat like a baby harp seal. Well, you have no idea where I worked, do you? In this part of Northern California, even a rabid rat, destined for the animal gas chamber, deserves humane treatment. No, I'm not kidding, it would have been a big deal to just bash its head in.

I took the box and cautiously advanced on the now very agitated rat. When I got close, it turned and ran. My mind wandered briefly because the rat had nowhere to go except into a corner of the building. Then my mind came back to reality with crystal-clear focus as the rat jumped against the building. It used the side of the building as a springboard to reverse its direction. With *Matrix*-like precision, the rat jumped directly at my privates, frothing mouth open, in one last, primal, insane, visceral assault to obtain freedom. In one smooth motion, without conscious thought, my training and expert reflexes caught the rat in the box as I slammed it against the wall. Sure. Truth is, I got really, really lucky. This was my moment of triumph. The crowd, now fifty strong, burst out in raucous applause. I took a bow and waited for animal control to respond. God it's good to be the hero!

After a few minutes, the animal control professionals arrived. I was relieved because they deal with this kind of stuff every day. No worries now! The animal control officer, a very experienced person, brought over a cage and explained the game plan. I would turn the box to the open door of the cage, and the rat would run in and be trapped. This logic sounded reasonable, so we gave it a go. Sure enough, the plan worked and the rat ran directly into the cage—and then immediately squeezed through the bars on the other side to freedom!

What happened next is the kind of stuff that legends are made of. Once again, without conscious thought, I reacted. I drew my baton, and in one smooth stroke, I bashed that rat's brains all over the sidewalk. I admit it was pretty ugly, but it had to be done! The next sound I heard still rings in my ears today. It was fifty people simultaneously gasping in horror. Mothers were shielding their children from the carnage. Others were literally yelling at me in anger. Some were just too shocked to speak. Sensing extreme danger, I did what anyone under similar circumstances would do. I bailed to my patrol car and got the hell out of there.

As I stated before, this part of Northern California can be really strange. I had no less than twenty people line up at the department to file complaints against me. I even made the front page of the newspaper the next day where my cruelty was cited and debated for some time. Right decision? Well, you can decide for yourself. I really upset a lot of people that day, not to mention the rat, and had to endure the ridicule of my peers for months.

Now, I don't mean to make light of having to deal with right and wrong issues. I'm using this story to make the point that sometimes you just can't win. What is right for you is wrong for others, and you just have to accept that. I know ethical decisions can be among the most vexing of problems, and in more serious circumstances, they can cause a tremendous amount of pain and suffering.

We have all heard the adage that it is better to be judged by twelve than carried by six. But that judgment can be cruel and humiliating. People who have no idea what we go through as warriors can sit for months debating the concept of right or wrong based on our actions during an event that took seconds to unfold, decisions we made based on information and circumstances available at the time and processed in split seconds. Knowing this judgment awaits us, how can we then be sure we have held ourselves to the highest standard in the application of our jobs?

So where does the answer lie? I believe we must follow our intuition. The little internal voice, or sixth sense, that guides us seldom lets us down. It is our second-guessing that gets us in trouble. Trust yourself and your training. Be honest in evaluating what you believe and how you act, and make changes wherever necessary. Above all, hold your head high, and hold yourself to the highest standards possible. Oh, and by the way, stay away from rabid rats!

I believe in the unconquerable
strength of my spirit.

# I believe in the unconquerable strength of my spirit.

# I believe in the unconquerable strength of my spirit!

*Great spirits have always encountered violent opposition from mediocre minds.*

—Albert Einstein, physicist

*All that spirits desire, spirits attain.*

—Kahlil Gibran,
"The Poet of Baalbek"

*No pessimist ever discovered the secret of the stars, or sailed to an uncharted land, or opened a new doorway for the human spirit.*

—Helen Keller, blind American
lecturer and author

# Shared Thoughts: Inner Strength

Remember Aron Ralston? This guy understands the inner strength of spirit. Aron embodies the true strength and resilience of a warrior. Aron is the brave soul who was hiking down a canyon in Colorado when a large boulder he was scaling moved, pinning his arm against a cliff wall. The 800-pound boulder had him trapped, limiting him to a painful, standing position with little room to move. For five days, Aron struggled to free himself, to no avail. He tried to rig a pulley to move the boulder, but that effort failed. He tried using a dull, cheap knife to chip away at the boulder, hoping to create a gap large enough to move his arm out. Impossible. Finally, after five days, with no more food and water, Aron made the choice to amputate his own arm in order to free himself.

I want you to imagine yourself in this position. His choices were clear: Take action or die. Could you do it? I would like to say I could, but until I was actually in that position . . . I shudder to think. Aron prepared for the operation. He used some clothing that he placed under his arm to soak up the blood. He tied a tourniquet as best he could around his arm and began to work. He deliberately broke the bones at his wrist and then sawed through his arm, with his dull knife, until he was free. The entire operation took about an hour. Yes, he felt the pain, but in his words, "I coped with it."

As if this was not enough, Aron now had to face hiking out of the canyon he had been trapped in for the last five days. He had to rig up a rope to repel down about sixty feet to get out of the canyon, bleeding profusely, with one arm! He had hiked about five miles, weak from a lack of food and water, still bleeding, when he ran into two other hikers who helped him to safety. Aron was airlifted to a hospital where he literally walked in under his own power. Does this sound unbelievable?

If you knew without an absence of doubt you had this capacity, this ability, this ironclad will to manifest your survival mechanism under the most extreme circumstances, imagine how powerful you could become. Imagine what you could accomplish.

I will tell you this: You do have this power. Every single man, woman, and child possesses this power. How else can you explain how a 120-pound woman can lift a burning car off of a child to save it? There are countless examples of this power manifested every day in our world. We usually chalk it up to a unique, impossible situation. It falls into the "that's amazing" category, and we pay it little attention because to acknowledge it means we would have to accept that which we think is impossible. The trick is to realize, believe with all your soul, that this power also resides within you. If you can make this transformation to realization, you will move beyond manifesting this power unconsciously during extreme events to being able to manifest it at will. Imagine!

I believe that if you asked Aron Ralston, he would tell you he is just a man, a regular guy. The 120-pound woman lifting a car to save her baby probably can't even open a jar of pickles absent the extreme event. But these people have experienced a higher level of consciousness that transcends what we believe to be "normal" or "possible." Struggle to move beyond limited thinking, and open yourself up to the reality that you are a limitless being! Visualize yourself overcoming "impossible" situations. Believe that this power resides within you. Believe you can call upon this power whenever you need it. Know it is true. Practice this positive thinking every moment of every day, and watch the marvelous results!

I will not let the things I cannot control anger me.

I will not let the things
I cannot control anger
me.

I will not let the
things I cannot con-
trol anger me!

*Angels and ministers of grace defend us.*
*Be thou a spirit of health, or goblin damned,*
*Bring with thee airs from heaven, or blasts from hell,*
*Be thy intents wicked, or charitable,*
*Thou com'st in such a questionable shape,*
*That I will speak to thee.*

—William Shakespeare, *Hamlet*

*If you are patient in one moment of anger, you will escape a hundred days of sorrow.*

—Chinese proverb

*How much more grievous are the consequences of anger than the causes of it.*

—Marcus Aurelius, Roman emperor
from 161 to 180 A.D.

*He who angers you, conquers you.*

—Elizabeth Kenny, Australian nurse
who advanced the treatment of polio

I will strive for personal change and growth.

# I will strive for personal change and growth.

# I will strive for personal change and growth!

*The rung of a ladder was never meant to rest upon, but only to hold a man's foot long enough to enable him to put the other somewhat higher.*

—Thomas Henry Huxley,
zoologist and advocate of Darwinism

*I do not think much of a man who is not wiser today than he was yesterday.*

—Abraham Lincoln, sixteenth president
of the United States

*There was that law of life, so cruel and so just, that one must grow or else pay more for remaining the same.*

—Norman Mailer, American author

*The journey is the reward.*

—Taoist saying

*If you don't like something, change it. If you can't change it, change your attitude. Don't complain.*

—Maya Angelou, American author

# Shared Thoughts:
# Personal Growth

I have talked a lot in this book about the ideals we should strive for in our role as warriors. It would be easy to come to the conclusion that we can reach our ultimate goals if we work hard every day. We should always seek our highest goals. However, we should also understand that perfection as a warrior is never quite within our grasp. Ask any warrior you respect if he has reached his ultimate potential. If he is not clouded with delusion, I can guarantee he will tell you he has not attained perfection, and he will be correct. Indeed, if they are honest with themselves, the great warriors will humbly tell you they are far from it. These warriors will tell you there is much more work to be done, much more they can do to improve themselves. This is the creed of a warrior: to constantly seek higher and higher levels of improvement.

If the highest level of becoming a warrior was easily obtained, it would cease to be worth pursuing. As I have stated before, the fact that this perfection is always seemingly beyond our reach should serve to fuel our inner fire to seek it. How exciting to know there is always room to improve. That striving for personal growth is limitless. It is what drives us to become better and better. It is the inspiration that gives us the strength to pick ourselves up even though we may experience failure. It allows us to believe we can continuously make improvements and constantly redefine who and what we are in our role as warriors.

Cultivate personal growth. Never settle for those experiences that make you feel comfortable and unchallenged. Get outside your comfort zone, and constantly push and challenge yourself. Do not fear failure; embrace it as a great teacher. Above all, struggle against those thoughts that limit you from becoming all that you want to be. Accept that you are a limitless being, capable of tremendous personal growth, and make up your mind right here and now to seek it!

# Final Thoughts

I want you to close your eyes and picture in your mind the soldier at Valley Forge, as he holds his musket in his bloody hands. He stands; barefoot in the snow, starved from lack of food, wounded from months of battle and emotionally scarred from the eternity away from his family surrounded by nothing but death and carnage of war.

He stands though, with fire in his eyes and victory on his breath. He looks at us now in anger and disgust and tells us this . . .

I gave you a birthright of freedom born in the Constitution and now your children graduate too illiterate to read it.

I fought in the snow barefoot to give you the freedom to vote and you stay at home because it rains.

I left my family destitute to give you the freedom of speech and you remain silent on critical issues, because it might be bad for business.

I orphaned my children to give you a government to serve you and it has stolen democracy from the people.

- It's the soldier, not the reporter, who gives you the freedom of the press.
- It's the soldier, not the poet, who gives you the freedom of speech.
- It's the soldier, not the campus organizer, who allows you to demonstrate.
- It's the soldier who salutes the flag, serves the flag, and whose coffin is draped with the flag that allows the protester to burn the flag.

*Lord, hold our troops in your loving hands. Protect them as they protect us. Bless them and their families for the selfless acts they perform for us in our time of need. I ask this in the name of Jesus, our Lord and Savior. Amen.*

—The Rev. John Hagee, president of Global
Evangelism Television

*To be a warrior is to learn to be genuine in every moment of your life.*

—Albert Einstein, physicist

*When young men seek to be like you, when lazy men resent you, when powerful men look over their shoulder at you, when cowardly men plot behind your back, when corrupt men wish you were gone and evil men want you dead, only then have you done your share.*

—Phil Messina–Modern Warrior

*To protect one's country and its helpless citizens against evil is righteous action. Spiritual power is the greatest force; it should be the bulwark behind every form of resistance and defense. The first line of action should be to use all spiritual and moral power possible to counter evil; and to strive to change the world's inclination to war and violence by removing the causes that strengthen evil—poverty and hunger, disease, injustice, greed and selfish interests. If, in the last, evil force has to be met with righteous force, the* **Bhagavad Gita** *advises the kshatriya, (the soldier), to not waver but fulfill bravely his God-given duty.*

—Paramahansa Yogananda,
founder of Self-Realization Fellowship

Each of us has within ourselves a spirit that cannot be defeated. Each of us must discover this aspect of ourselves and upon its discovery, go forth to complete our duties in this life. Our capacity for personal growth is limitless, and we must strive constantly to re-create the grandest vision of what we wish to become. It is my sincere hope that this book begins to open a door of self-discovery to the warrior spirit within you, helping it to grow ever stronger. When you look deep within yourself, your service and dedication to duty will be rewarded in ways it is difficult to imagine. Through introspection, these rewards will be realized and will continue to help you grow stronger. May your journey as a warrior draw you ever closer to the infinite source of spirit, and may God bless you for your selfless sacrifice and service.

—Rodger

# *Biography*

Rodger Ruge is a recently retired police officer (after 18 years of service) trained in the martial arts. He is a Police Defensive Tactics Instructor, a Weaponless Defense/Martial Arts Instructor, and a Certified Stress Management Trainer. His new company, Ready Force Inc. (www.readyforce.net), offers training and consulting in Use of Force to police officers and private security personnel. Beyond that, Rodger has designed a 24-hour training program in fitness, nutrition, and stress management for law enforcement personnel, and has recently been tapped by the California POST (Peace Officer Standards and Training) Master Instructor Program (the highest level of law enforcement instruction in California), for which he will begin teaching in March 2005.

Rodger is also co-founder of Police Health, a business dedicated to providing stress management training to emergency services personnel (www.policehealth.us). He lives in Windsor, CA.

Rodger is available for seminars, lectures, and private consulting. You may reach him by e-mail at *readyforce@comcast.net*, or visit his Web site at *www.readyforce.net*.

# Coming Attractions

Rodger is currently developing a CD to complement *The Warrior's Mantra*. This CD will contain guided narration exercises to relax the mind and take the mantras learned in this book deep into the subconscious. Please visit his Web site for additional information, *www.readyforce.net*.

# Notes

---

# NOTES

# NOTES

# NOTES

# NOTES

# NOTES